MW00908065

COLLEGE INTERVIEW ESSENTIALS

So....You Think You Can Interview?

❖ ❖ ❖

Peggy Nash Marx & Kyrie O'Connor

TwoBig Publishing Company

CIC – www.collegeinterviewcounselors.com
www.careerinterviewcoaches.com

First Edition
Literary Editor: Michael Clive
Cover Design: Mara Nash
Cartoon: Max Farinato
ISBN-10: 1530137047
ISBN 13: 9781530137046
Library of Congress Control Number: 2016902955
CreateSpace Independent Publishing Platform
North Charleston, South Carolina

So why do you want to attend Skylark University?

Table of Contents

CHAPTER 1

Can you have a Conversation?

❖ ❖ ❖

CHAPTER 1

Can you have a Conversation?

❖ ❖ ❖

"Hey!"

"Hey!"

Wazzup?

Nuthin. U?

Hangin'

Movie?

Yeah.

Landmark. 8

There.

Bummed. ☹

Huh?

College.

Huh?

Applications.

Seriously?

Yeah.

Problem?

Essays/Interviews 😬

So?

So?

What do I say? 

Say?

For what?

Interview. I never had an interview…..

What do I say? 

How am I going to get in?

Taken from any teenager's smartphone, this dialogue highlights not only the anxiety associated with the college process, but the monosyllabic conversations typical of a young generation locked in a technological, texting age. Yes, Jenny (above) communicated to Doug that she would meet him at the movies and at a certain theatre. Yes… she acknowledges her stress at completing her college applications – most specifically her anxieties about successfully "nailing" her interview. But does this communication reveal if she has the skills to competently deliver that unique conversation -- the interview -- which can prove critical for college and graduate school admissions, not to mention future career pursuits? Jenny is young and is just embarking on her entrance into an adult, mature, and stressful world of present day competition in society. She likely requires specific training and a focused skill set equipping her to carry on an articulate, impactful interview – necessary elements in the ultimate achievement of her goals.

Is there any wonder she is concerned about pulling off an Impressive Interview? Or worried about her abilities to carry on a conversation? Her communication with Doug reveals that she has grown up in an age of one-word cadences, acronyms, and silent texts. She has answered questions in a classroom and on written tests. She may have voiced terse responses to parental inquiries. But, carry on a reasoned, interactive conversation? One that is meant to be self-supportive? Informative yet succinct? An elevator speech of sorts? That is a tall order for a first-timer out of the gate.

The impetus for writing this handbook stems from the authors' combined 20 years' experience interviewing college and job applicants and as chairs of a top-level academic institution's alumni interview program. Our method of interview training, with an emphasis on revealing individual potential, is delivered through private consultations and workshops. These platforms embody our initiative to guide younger generations in the art of communication and self-marketing. With this manual, we aim to help students succeed on the college application stage. We offer calm, solid guidance on how to make the college interview work for each candidate.

Starting with the release of mobile phones complete with text messaging capabilities, young people's interview skills have eroded while their technological skills have increased exponentially. This inability to use conversation as a marketing tool is directly linked to our electronically-based and texting-focused societies.

By the way… how many phone calls did you receive today? How many texts?

Reality reveals the Truth

Not surprisingly, young people's reliance upon texting has affected the way they speak in interviews. This has manifested itself into what we refer to as monosyllabic interrogations. Here are examples of what was and what could have been:

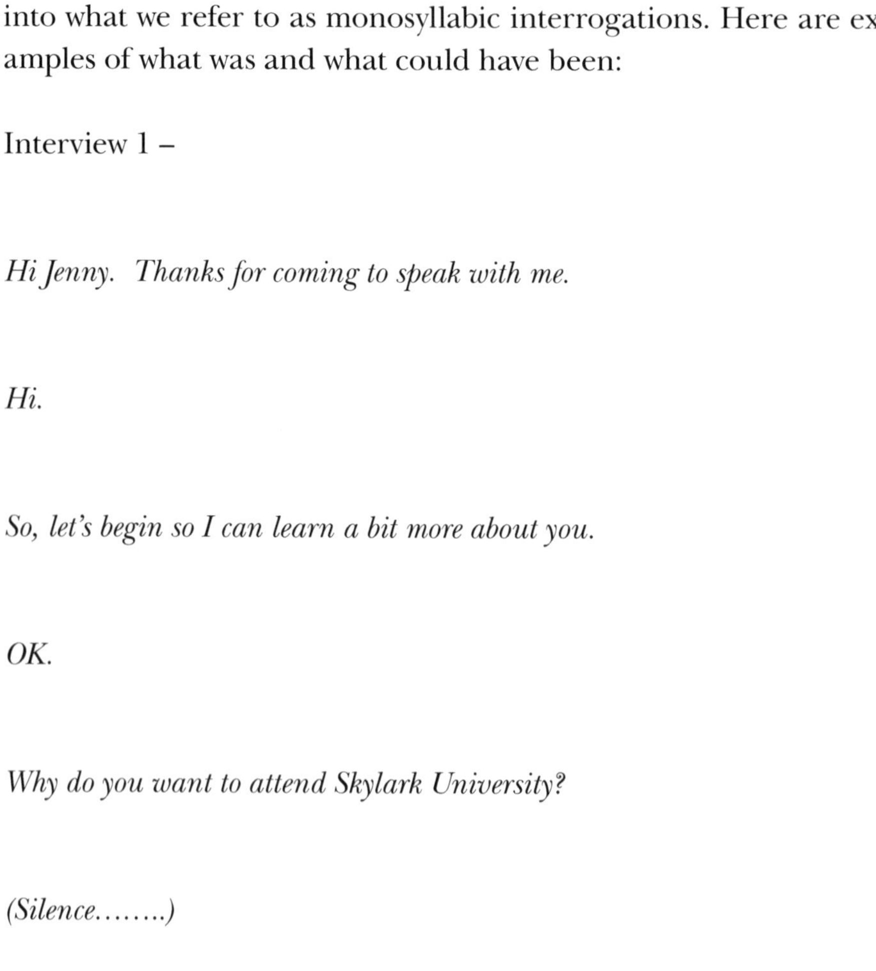

Interview 1 –

Hi Jenny. Thanks for coming to speak with me.

Hi.

So, let's begin so I can learn a bit more about you.

OK.

Why do you want to attend Skylark University?

(Silence……..)

Um……my cousin attended the school and told me it was great.

(Waiting…………nothing)

OK – tell me something about yourself. How was your high school experience?
(Moments of silence…)

Are there highlights of your time there?

High School was fine. Like…..I had friends, good teachers.
(I have no idea what to say…..)

Is there any subject in the news that interests you?

Uh……No, not really. Like, you mean, famous people?
(I don't think she knows about JT)
No.

What do you feel are your weaknesses?

Umm……I have never been really good at math. So…. like….. I am so glad that like I never have to take a math class again.

I have been asking you a few questions. Do you have any questions for me?

No...

Interview 2

Hi Jenny – thanks for meeting with me.

Thank you for taking the time to interview me.

So, let's begin so I can learn a bit more about you.

That sounds great.

Why do you want to attend Skylark University?

I travelled to Skylark University this past summer for an official tour although I had visited my cousin who is a student at Skylark a few times before. I've been lucky to have a member of the family go out into the college world before me. She has been able to guide me on my college search. But it turned out that even though I visited other schools on my tour, I personally felt so comfortable on Skylark's campus and just hope that I will be able to attend next year. When I visited I met Professor Dunbar, Dean of the Biology Department. He showed me around the new science building and explained how Skylark would offer me an opportunity to set off on my goals to do cellular research. He explained that Skylark University allows undergraduate students the time to work alongside graduate students on specific projects! That way, I can learn from my peers as well as from my professors and through individual study. From the get go I will be involved in tangible, productive research – something I hope to pursue to tackle disease.

Sounds exciting – I can only be grateful that you and others are trying to protect society.

Can you tell me something about your high school experience? Are there highlights of your time there?

I think I've had a great high school experience. Our town only has one high school, so it is extremely large – thousands of kids. Even though I was usually with a certain group for my classes, as many of us took the same level courses, I loved constantly being able to meet new friends in theatre, sports or just in the lunch room. I don't think my school was as cliquey as I've heard some places can be. Since I was involved with the newspaper all four years that also gave me an opportunity to report on and know about so many activities going on in the school. I was able to hear if some of the students were upset about something or were working on a new program. Hopefully I will be able to work on the news website at Skylark as well – it is a great way to always know what is going on.

I agree. I worked on Skylark's newspaper (in my day it was a newspaper) while I was there as well. It was wonderful and actually ended up linking me with my internship position in Boston during my senior year.

What do you feel are your weaknesses?

Well, I must admit that I have never loved math – not because I did not do well in the courses, but because I never fully understood the science of numbers like some other kids do. However, I was able to keep up with them because I do understand the value of math in everything – science, business, household needs. So I know I will never be a math teacher or mathematician. But I know that I can hold my own and use what I have learned in whichever field I pursue.

Good for you. I agree – you will do fine in whatever you pursue. (The interviewer already likes Jenny and identifies with her.)

So is there any global issue that you are interested in?

My mother is from Israel and my father is Egyptian. We have relatives still living in both countries - so you can imagine that we try to stay on top of what is going on in the Middle East as well as with U.S. activities in the region. It is rare that my family does not talk about politics at the dinner table. Sometimes our conversations are quite heated. But I have always known that it is more important to argue with words and attempt negotiation than harm people for whatever reason. It is so sad that religion and tribal warfare and power hungry individuals have caused so much destruction on our planet.

I can tell that you and I could have hour-long discussions about so much that goes on in this world. You must have had a very interesting youth. Kudos to your parents for engaging you in all that goes on in our volatile world.

I have been asking you a bunch of questions. Do you have any questions for me?

Yes, actually. I was wondering what you felt was your greatest experience at Skylark University?

Well, as you can see I went to Skylark University many years ago. But I can still recall how thrilled I was to be able to participate in so many of the school's activities, even though I studied engineering. Rather than being pegged as a "nerdy" engineer, I auditioned for and acted in many of the school's musical productions. I also was part of the debate team and travelled to other schools where, by chance, I often saw my friends from high school. I loved the spirit of Skylark and, even though I did not know a lot about football, I learned about the game from my friends and did not miss one home game, having bought season tickets to cheer on our guys.

Then, back in engineering, we were one of the first classes to work on a robotics project and, as you may know, robotics is now the hot topic in the engineering world. So I feel that Skylark was cutting edge, even back in my day.

...OK, I think I have taken you down my memory lane enough...

Sounds great – thanks for that vivid picture. Have you been able to maintain friendships you made on campus throughout your adult years?

Most definitely. Actually I ended up marrying someone from Skylark whom I had not even met while we were on campus together. And we stay in touch with a lot of old friends from college days.

The "good" interview scenario reveals the candidate's maturity - the passage from childhood to adulthood. The interviewer is impressed with this candidate's ability to articulate her goals and aspirations for her future. This will result in a positive write-up.

These two sample scenarios may seem that they could not have come out of the same applicant's mouth. But our experience and techniques have shown that anyone can learn how to improve upon their interview skills. If reticent, one can learn how to speak softly but reveal much. If boisterous, one can express enthusiasm yet learn how to listen as well.

Life Skill

Most importantly, interviewing is a life skill. Your college admissions interview is the first of many conversations that will play a pivotal role in the direction and quality of your life... learning interviewing skills before high school graduation can help you take charge of your future. Bad interview habits start early and tend to be self-reinforcing. So, the sooner a young person gains a strong interview skill base, the better she will be equipped to capitalize on future opportunities. The sooner an individual becomes a confident interviewer, the more primed he will be for future interviewing events for:

- Internships
- Scholarships
- Graduate Schools
- Jobs/Career

CHAPTER 2

The Rub

❖ ❖ ❖

CHAPTER 2

The Rub

❖ ❖ ❖

The Key to Having the Conversation is Preparation

The performance differential between the two interviews in Chapter 1 is dramatic. Having an interview is akin to being on stage. Although the interview is designed to reveal to the Admissions Committee who you really are and how your personality melds with your written application, you must learn to adapt your behavior to the needs of the interview at hand. That means using the opportunity to market yourself in the best possible light. It also means that you must appreciate the interviewer's time and, by being prepared for the task at hand, make the interviewer's job of writing your review as easy as possible.

In Scenario 2, Jenny has prepared herself to reveal as much positive information as possible in a limited time period. She is not just waiting for the questions she practiced to be asked; Jenny has shaped her answers to many questions to be descriptive of herself and pique the interest of her interviewer. She comes across as sincere and engaged in a meaningful, albeit brief, conversation. Preparation allows her to manage the conversation to her advantage. Jenny set the stage for her Impressive Interview by following the steps outlined in this book.

In contrast, Scenario 1 exemplifies how an unprepared Jenny reacts to questions. She has not planned her answers to any of an interviewer's queries, nor determined what she would like to communicate – the keys to an Impressive Interview. And, like many of her generation, the unprepared Jenny has reason to be concerned.

The Interview – Perhaps the Most Difficult Part of the Application

Unlike a written application, the interview does not allow for any " lifelines." Jenny's high school academics have presumably prepared her to write a cogent essay. And – no worries – those essays can be proofed by her parents, her teachers, and anyone else who accepts the responsibility to "perfect" her written words. But what about those interviews? Nothing in high school has prepared her for having a self-marketing (forward thinking, self-promoting - yet humble) discussion about her attributes. She is on her own and, not surprisingly, she is not ready to have an Impressive Interview.

The Rub

It has been famously said that "one doesn't have a second chance to make a first impression." Jenny and her peers have one shot, one chance to succeed at a live interview. What are the odds of Jenny's having a positive interview? She has never had an interview. She does not want to have stage fright. She wants to make sure that her interview highlights her individual virtues, accomplishments and aspirations. Her goal is to have the interviewer leave their meeting as her advocate, writing a powerful piece supporting Jenny's admission to the school to which she has applied.

The common mindset is that the interview part of a college application is merely fluff – PR – unimportant. In this day and age, that perception is far from reality. Yet even within that mindset, can candidates that apply to schools take that chance? Colleges are looking for **reasons to reject applicants and <u>a negative interview can tip the scales into the reject pile.</u>** Each generation going forward realizes that, with the mounting number of applications submitted to each school, SOMETHING must differentiate the thousands of kids from each other and help the admissions committee determine who should gain a seat in that freshman class. The Impressive You can be achieved by utilizing the methodology designed by this book's authors.

Parental Support / Irony of Blind Love

Parents of non-communicative teenagers may recognize the necessity for interview preparation. They may reason, correctly, that if they have never witnessed their son/daughter have a meaningful conversation, the skills to do so will not miraculously appear at the time of an interview.

However, it is ironic that parents of talkative teenagers are convinced – are positive and confident - that their cherished ones will excel in the interview. Yet, realistically, the over talkers are just as needy for guidance and preparation as the under talkers. It is too late to worry about a miscue or a less than stellar performance after that one-time interview has taken place.

According to the Daily Beast:

> *... most parents think their son or daughter is wonderful and will give a great interview; parents are often poor judges of their children. Never assume you will give a good interview unless you are coached.*
>
> The Daily Beast (http://campusbeast.com/your-guide-to-college-interviews)

As in sports, academics, acting, or any competitive arena – "winging it" will not do. It may allow for survival of the interrogation, but it will likely not result in an impactful conversation or an Impressive Interview.

What Can Be Done?

The following chapters provide you with the tools you need to perform more effectively in interviews. Interview skills can and should be developed early in life, as they will be called upon for college, internship, scholarship, job and career applications for many years to come.

Before getting into actual preparation, it is important, as in all things, to understand the purpose of an activity – the end game. So, first, let's ask: Why do schools hold interviews at all?

CHAPTER 3

What Is All the Fuss About?

❖ ❖ ❖

CHAPTER 3

What Is All the Fuss About?

❖ ❖ ❖

Facts:

Interviews for admission are offered and encouraged at:

95% of the top 75 Colleges
88% of the top 25 Universities

(College rankings U.S. News and World Report; statistics per college websites)

These numbers are probably higher than you imagined they would be. And the key words are "offered and encouraged." In many situations, the interview is an optional element of the application. But, as you will realize after digesting the chapters of this book, it is only to an applicant's advantage to accept the offer to be interviewed.

In prior years, the student checked off the option to have a personal interview on a preliminary contact form. However, with formats ever-changing, some schools now only allow the applicant to opt in for the interview later in the game – often after the written application has been received and registered into the system – on a status check email or the like. Whatever the case, since more often than not the interviews are **evaluative**...for your own benefit, accept the interview offers from your schools of choice. And note, it is nearly impossible to be granted an interview slot after the initial offers have been extended. So, be aware and careful about all correspondence sent to you by a particular school. It may not be the offer you are waiting for – a seat in the freshman class – but the offer guarantees you another voice in your application. And, although the interview *alone* cannot place you in the admit pile, it has the ability to convince the admissions staff of your **potential** – a key element for acceptance by a university.

Institutions' Perspectives

This is what Colleges say on their websites about the interview:

> *"An interview is a great way for a member of the Admission Committee to get to know you on a more personal basis than what your grade point average, rank in class and SAT or ACT scores reveal."*

> *"Treat this as a job interview, as it is an important piece of our holistic review."*

> *"An interview is our chance to get to know you as a person rather than just a collection of papers."*

> *"...putting a face and a personality to an application is very helpful. We're most interested in learning what you think about, what kind of person you are, what makes you curious. It's a two-way street: we want you to ask questions, too!"*

> *"….we strongly recommend a personal interview. Without one, some students may be at a disadvantage at the time of admissions selections."*

> *"To give you the chance to address any issues in your application that are best explained in a personal conversation."*

> *"We want to know what you're passionate about, what your dream career is, and what you've been doing to make it happen. This is your chance to set yourself apart from other applicants."*

A final quote - one Ivy League school admits on its website:

> *"In fact, last year, of eligible applicants, we admitted 10.8% of those who had an interview but only 1% of those who chose not to interview."*

With the advent of common apps, universal apps, and the like, more and more schools -- especially the most selective ones -- ask for supplemental essays in an effort to deeply understand candidates and their commitment to the university. The written essays can offer the Admissions Departments a glimpse as to how an individual will fit into the culture of their school. Furthermore, additional essays glean the commitment of the applicant who is willing to take time and thought to complete supplemental essays. It is too easy to push a button to submit a canned common app to a myriad of schools – schools which were never visited, analyzed or coveted by the applicant.

So too, a candidate can sincerely reveal his commitment to the application process by preparing for a specific school's interview. Once a candidate has succeeded in having an

Impressive Interview, he can feel that he has put his best foot forward and addressed all elements of the application to the best of his ability.

John Birney, Senior Associate Director of Admission at Johns Hopkins shares:

> *"....for a kid who is on the bubble, where the decision could go either way, a fantastic interview with an alumnus could make the difference. " But he also adds, "The flip side is also true. A kid who comes across as arrogant or nasty or ill-informed about the college can trigger a negative interview report. It is rare that it happens, but it does. And when it does, it can be what tips the scale."*
>
> The Daily Beast: "Do College Interviews Count?"

Remember, all of the top schools have far more qualified applicants than they can handle. And if you are a "no show" to an alumni interview – or refuse one – you can be sure that your actions are passed on to the Admissions Office.

Authors' Personal Experiences as Chairs

During our twenty-year tenure as Chairs of an Alumni Interview Committee, we interfaced with the Admissions Office and were kept apprised of the purpose of the interview program. The Admissions Committee would continuously update us on what they hoped to learn from students' interviews. The Admissions Office frequently held workshops for national and international interview volunteers. Along with keeping the interviewers abreast of new developments, the workshops – replete with handbooks, power point presentations and the like – imparted the role the interviews play in the evaluation process.

Actual students' files (names had been changed) were distributed and discussed. Along with a rating system on standardized test scores, extracurricular activities, essay expression, background and high school attended, the **file also always included a rating based on the interviewer's write-up.** Make no mistake: The write-up alone cannot catapult a person into the accepted pile. But encouraging words from an interviewer who speaks with multiple applicants each season, can get the Admissions committee "on your side."

A fellow alumni interviewer from Yale comments:

> *"I've been on an admissions committee and an evaluator of essays. So many well-qualified applicants have comparable credentials and any distinguishing factor, such as good performance in an interview, can become the deciding factor."*

Skills Learned Early Come in Handy

Undergraduate college and university admissions offices' evaluation techniques mirror, albeit lag behind, graduate programs' methods for admissions. As graduate programs are placing greater emphases on the interview over a written application, undergraduate college and university admissions departments may be expected to follow a similar trend. Schools are seeking personal expression – in the form of live interactions – conversations. This element is key to determining an individual's potential at an institution of higher learning, a community or a work environment.

In a Wall Street Journal article entitled "Want to Get Into Business School? Write Less" (WSJ 7/3/14), reporter Adams

Rubensfire, refutes the lackadaisical attitude held by many towards the interview. His research indicates the increasing power of the interview in the application process. He notes that whereas, in the past, business school applications required the writing of multiple essays for admission, the current thinking reduces the number of required essays and places the interview higher on the evaluative scale for the applicant.

> *"……. Schools say the changes reflect a renewed focus on interviews, videos and other live interactions to get a sense of how applicants really think – and not what admissions officers want to hear."*
>
> *Rubensfire goes on to report, "Harvard Business School last year asked applicants to provide only one essay, and even made that optional…In 2004, the school asked applicants to complete six essay questions. Since then, said Leopold (HBS managing director of admissions and financial aid), one-on-one interviews have given officials a better sense of whether applicants are Harvard material." She further reveals, "The exercise (the interview) showcases applicants' ability to think quickly, which is more appropriate than having months to craft responses to personal essays, and more in line with the type of deadlines M.B.A.'s will face in the classroom and in their careers."*

So, in conclusion – why do many colleges and universities "offer and encourage interviews?"

- They do it to glean an applicant's personality, drive and reason for applying to a particular school.
- They want to substantiate if the conversational ability of the interviewee is consistent with the candidate's submitted paperwork. As mentioned above, the written words can be

worked on by multiple adults, including parents and hired consultants. The interviews can only become Impressive by virtue of how young candidates present themselves.

- The admissions committee wants to be sure it is pulling together a class of a well comprised group of individuals - diverse, yet fitting together into a cohesive whole.
- The interview allows the applicant to shine in a visible, live arena.

This is what all the fuss is about…..

CHAPTER 4

The Skinny on the Interview Process

❖ ❖ ❖

CHAPTER 4

The Skinny on the Interview Process

❖ ❖ ❖

Where and When Interviews Take Place

Campus interviews are conducted during the senior summer (prior to a candidate's senior year of high school), or in the fall of senior year. Many families tour schools at these times and are able to arrange on-campus meetings along with reservations for information session and/or walking campus tours. By the time early decision deadlines come around (November), it is rare that a school will have the staff availability for on-campus interviews.

Smaller colleges are usually more amenable to offering one-on-one campus meetings with students than are larger universities. Yet these days, due to the sheer number of applicants, most colleges rely on their alumni to speak with candidates in a local setting.

Do NOT underestimate the power or influence of the local alumni volunteer interviewers. Whereas it may be true that the local interviewer will not be able to gloss over a weak transcript or resume, or have the admissions committee disregard lower than expected test scores, the local interviewer's write-up becomes an integral part of the application file and, as mentioned before, is **evaluative**.

Who are these alumni and why do they take their time to interview potential students? Volunteers offer services to their schools in a variety of ways. They may attend meetings and be appointed to alumni boards to involve themselves in school policy or strategic planning. Others enjoy keeping in touch with the younger generation. By interviewing potential candidates the alums feel they can help maintain their schools standing by providing input on the candidates to be accepted to their alma mater.

Some alumni interview programs make a great effort to match interviewers with applicants' stated areas of academic interest. If a young person decides that medicine is her calling, the interviewer might be a local doctor. If engineering is the dominant interest, the university might call upon a local engineer to speak to the applicant about this career-focused study and its relationship to the current industry. Who knows? You may follow up with the interviewer for an internship in the future.....

Certain schools have upperclassmen speak to applicants to offer their candid opinions about how the interviewee will fit into the school environment. Don't be cavalier about these younger interviewers. Although close in age to the applicants themselves, these students are loyal to their school and most interested in the fabric of the student body. They are hardly pushovers and must be taken seriously by the high school candidate. Treat them with respect, as you would the older interviewer – not as someone who you are confident you can WOW with your self-proclaimed charisma.

Most importantly, applicants must maintain a **positive attitude** about each school with which they are interviewing. You want the interviewer to appreciate your distinctive characteristics and become an advocate of your application.

This is not rocket science. Let's play the scene forward –

You are a fly on the wall of the Admissions "War Room." First the Admissions reader reviews an applicant's paperwork, including the write-up from the local interviewer. This admissions officer is not fully supportive of the candidate, so places the individual in the "Maybe" pile. Once the Admissions Committee convenes around their conference table, finalizing admissions decisions (admitted, denied or deferred), the reader can bring up the supportive letter written by the volunteer interviewer. In this particular theoretical case, the interviewer has been offering her services to the school for years. Therefore, she is considered an experienced judge of student potential. The admissions staff hears the words from "boots on the ground" and is persuaded to admit the previously questionable candidate.

This is not fiction. Rather it proves the importance of being at the top of your game for all interviews – reach schools and safeties alike.

CHAPTER 5

Interview Training - No Pain No Gain

❖ ❖ ❖

CHAPTER 5

Interview Training - No Pain No Gain

❖ ❖ ❖

So, what is the framework by which one can prepare for an interview? An analogy of a cricket bat comes to mind:

If the interviewer handed you a cricket bat and asked you to play for 30 minutes, would you be able to complete the task? You can run, jump, hold a bat. But you do not know the rules of the game, and, most importantly, you do not have the skill set from hours of practice to know how to win the game.

So too, you can type and speak English. You can answer questions. But how would that translate into an Impressive Interview? Your interview is **not an interrogation** with the objective being survival. You want to have a **conversation** with the interviewer – a dialogue that interests the interviewer, highlights your individual talents, discusses your civic engagement, demonstrates your academic and intellectual assets, and leaves the interviewer wholly supporting your application and cheering you on to the finish line.

Journalists covering the education space, further reveal a refocusing of admissions offices in their evaluative techniques. It does not suffice to list stellar accomplishments. Rather, a candidate must be able to communicate what they have done thus far, and what they hope to pursue in the future, to benefit society as a whole. In a recent Washington Post article, Jennifer Wallace and Lisa Heffernan covered the state-of-the-art college application environment: To get into college, a Harvard report advocates kindness instead of overachieving.

> *..."a new report released today by Making Caring Common, a project of the Harvard Graduate School of Education, takes a major step in trying to change the college admissions process to make it more humane, less super-human."*

> *..."Yes, we want students who have achieved in and out of the classroom, but we are also looking for things that are harder to quantify, [like] authentic intellectual engagement and a concern for others and the common good," explains Jeremiah Quinlan, dean of undergraduate admissions at Yale University...*

> *..."the University of Virginia is also in agreement with the report. 'We support Turning the Tide because we philosophically agree with many of the principle points in the document, [like] promoting, encouraging, and developing good citizenship, strong character, personal responsibility, [and] civic engagement in high school students," says Gregory Roberts, the school's dean of admissions.*

Especially in the current admissions atmosphere, which is attempting to qualify and value citizenship, the interview is a perfect opportunity for candidates to speak about their contributions to a community and society as a whole.

So, let's get started. A quick read of our primer will reveal the background story, skills and training elements which will send applicants on the road to have an Impressive Interview.

Throw the Interviewer a Bone

The age of Facebook has propelled our youth to draw attention to their individual achievements and events. "Look at me! – Look how happy I am! Look how many friends I have! Don't you want to be a part of my group? Be enthralled by my aura?"

So goes the screen dialogue of pictures, cute sayings, joke cartoons and emojis. But what about, how the person contributes to the group? How does the candidate add value to a living, breathing community – such as a college campus? The Facebook generation is all about me and I. So how does that impact our interview?

It's true that the interviewer wants to learn more about you. However, the interviewer wants to envision how you will engage with your fellow students on the college campus. What would you bring to the table? What makes you deserving of that freshman seat? Will your personality and talents adjust to and mold well into the campus community? Will you be that piece of the puzzle that fits into the whole while maintaining your individualism?

In the interview, it is most important that you **brand** yourself... that you define what makes you that missing puzzle piece. What will be your **value-add** to the community at large? Why will the campus function better with you than without you? This branding will be further discussed and outlined in Chapter 6 - The Impressive You–Your Brand.

In order to answer the question about your value add, it is essential that you do your homework: **research the place for which you are interviewing.** Whether it be a college or (in your future) a company or a professional practice, you must know as much as you can about the coveted place so that you can address how you will best fit in. Be sure you are acquainted with the school's academics; that you know about its extracurricular activities – clubs, special groups, location, opportunities, academic structure, unique departments, etc. Once in the interview, you will be speaking with someone who is passionate about the school to which you are applying. In the case of an alumnus, why else would the volunteer spend his or her valuable time interviewing potential students?

When you have been matched with an interviewer, take some time to **research the person with whom you will be speaking.** That graduate might be profiled on LinkedIn, Facebook, or under a Google search. The more you know about your interviewer, the better your conversation can be – knowledge is power. The person you will be meeting with will be less of a stranger if you know something about him/her. Also, although the interview is an arena where the alum will be able to paint a picture of you for the admissions committee, you must come prepared with questions of your own to substantiate your interest in the school to which you are applying and to evoke the interviewer's interest in you. Be equipped **to carry on an exchange of information (the conversation)** with the interviewer.

Please remember that these preparatory skills will be repeated when the time comes for job or internship interviews. Later in life you will use the same research skills to assess the companies or organizations for which you hope to work. You must be knowledgeable on their structure and culture so you and your interviewer can ascertain whether or not you are a good fit – just as you try to find the right fit for your college years. The college interview must be treated with the same seriousness of purpose as a job interview and vice versa. The skills you train for on college admissions interviews will be enhanced by your maturity and experience at the career level.

So, we have determined that in order to be successful in the interview, you must brand yourself. You also must perform your due diligence to learn who it is that you will be meeting with and what you will be speaking about (the school.) Now let's return to actual examples from our years of interviewing competitive candidates to provide an overview on the "Rules of Engagement."

Interview Tips

Be on Time

How do you achieve the goal of getting the interviewer to be supportive of your candidacy? Most high school students, especially by their senior year, are extremely busy. It is unusual that you will be waiting around for the phone to ring or for the email to arrive, telling you when to meet for a college interview. Many interviewers offer the candidate a few meeting times so that schedules are coordinated. Even if you are "booked" at the offered times, figure out a way to apologize to your coach, your music teacher, your friends, your family, and grab one of the times offered. Remember that the interviewer is interviewing you and many other candidates; he too is busy and has a life. So, appreciate the times offered and make sure you are able to make the date. And, to show your initial enthusiasm and respect for the interview opportunity, arrive 10 minutes early to the appointed venue. Research the location to ensure that you will arrive at the correct place. Also, since the meeting is often scheduled for only 30 minutes and you should have a lot to say in that time, you want to be ready to go as soon as the interviewer is set up so as not to waste any precious exposure to your potential advocate.

Scene 1

Mrs. Smith has engaged in an email correspondence with Jesse in order to set a date for Jesse's college interview. Mrs. Smith and Jesse agree to meet at Starbucks on Route 1 in Greenwich, CT. The day and time have arrived and Mrs. Smith leaves her job early in order to speak with Jesse before she has to pick up her own child at a soccer game.

Mrs. Smith sits down at Starbucks with pad and pen at the ready. While waiting, she looks down at her phone to catch up on the day's emails. Fifteen minutes after the arranged time, Mrs. Smith sees no sign of any high school student. A few seconds later her phone rings. Jesse, out of breath, apologizes profusely. She settled into the wrong Starbucks. It is true that there is more than one Starbucks on Route 1 in Greenwich – as a matter of fact there are 5 Starbucks in town, three of which are on Route 1. Mrs. Smith agrees to wait for Jesse for a few more minutes until she arrives. However, Mrs. Smith is already questioning Jesse's organizational skills. And Mrs. Smith can only allow 40 minutes for Jesse's interview. Jesse finally arrives. But she has now lost 20 minutes of valuable interview time – time she cannot retrieve.

Perhaps, in reality, both are at fault for the ambiguity about which Starbucks location was meant for the meeting. However, Jesse is the one being judged – it was incumbent on her to do the advance planning as to the precise location.

Be sure you determine -- perhaps with MapQuest or Waze -- the exact address of the meeting place. It is not good enough to **think** you know which Starbucks your interviewer is referring to. It is important to arrive 10 minutes early to the meeting. That way you are raring to go as soon as you and the interviewer have connected and you are maximizing your face-to-face with the school representative who is going to **submit a write-up for your file. Don't brag or overstate; be humble; know how to filter your dialogue.**

Scene 2:

Peter arrived at the interview on time and seemed excited to talk all about himself.

Why should the Admissions Committee of Skylark University accept you over another candidate?

"I am a very good student and I know that Skylark takes students with good grades. I am particularly good at math and this year the school had to come up with a special math course for me since I have taken all of the regular and Honors and AP courses my school offered. Actually I have taken 15 AP courses and, over the summers, I have gone to the local college to take other academic courses. I got 5's on all of my AP exams and I am a national Merit Scholar.

When I was a kid I went to Kumon Math. Then I played piano and I still practice a few hours each day. I am applying to all of the Ivy League Schools and your school is one of the ones I am applying to which is good academically even though it is not Ivy League.

And so it went on for 30 minutes. The interviewer heard all about Peter's brilliance, his academic prowess, and how he thought he went through all of his school years "the right way." Now he felt it was time for him to be admitted to all of the schools because he had done everything right and aced all of his grades and standardized tests. What more could any school want? The bragging scenario is a booby trap for any student and is something that must be avoided.

By the end of the meeting, the interviewer was exhausted. Peter had done all of the talking. Although his interview was hardly monosyllabic, this was not a conversation but a monologue. Rather than exhibiting any humility, or acknowledging how fortunate he was to have been offered the opportunity to take advanced courses, not to mention his genetic brainpower, Peter spent the entire time shining his medals. Humility may be counter-intuitive for young interviewees. However, there are ways to discuss achievements and accomplishments and still be humble.

By referencing that Skylark was not Ivy League he was revealing that, if admitted, he would settle for Skylark but probably only as a last resort. This is a blatant statement where the interviewee did not filter the words that were coming out of his mouth and alienated the interviewer. Just like the miscues that occur in texting conversations, you have to be sure that your words are correctly interpreted. If in doubt, keep your thoughts to yourself.

Now it was time to write up this applicant. The interviewer had nothing to say...Peter's written application tells the admissions committee all of the academic highlights he just discussed. No one from the admissions department wants a rehash of his grades or test scores. The interviewer may have felt confident that Peter could succeed academically at Skylark. But she did not feel that he would be a welcome member to the community. Her write-up could only detract from his application, not support it.

Determine which points you want to make

You must focus your answers to the interviewer's questions on points you want the interviewer to walk away with and what you hope she will write about! Peter spent the entire time talking about how wonderful he was. He certainly showed his arrogance, but hardly how he integrates with others from his peer group, or what he is interested in doing on this earth. He thought he was going to impress.

The irony is that Peter probably walked away from the interview thinking that he had done well. Like others, he assumed that since he can talk about himself and his accomplishments, he can do well on an interview.

Know what you will try to communicate in the hopes that the interviewer will become your advocate.

You may recall the section, "Throw the Interviewer a Bone." Since each interviewer must speak and write up many candidates, you must try to make the interviewer's job easier, rather than more difficult. If an interviewer had an interesting -- maybe even enlightening -- conversation with you, he will have no problem remembering what makes you unique and submitting a complimentary, supportive review. Make the interviewer's job easy by preparing yourself with answers to questions and knowing how you will incorporate aspects about your experiences and personality and drive into the conversation. (More on Impressive Interview points later in Chapter 6.)

Dress for Success

We are always asked how one should dress for the interview. A rule of thumb is: "Dress as if you were going to visit your grandmother. If you think you look good, go put on something else!" Result of this approach - goal met. You have dressed "neutrally" and the interviewer does not remark upon your attire in his evaluation.

Concentrate on the Task at Hand

Most of the local alumni interviews are held in public places – often in a Starbucks or restaurant. (Schools no longer allow a young candidate to be alone with an alum in a home or private office. This is to insure that there is no unnecessary uneasiness – except normal nervousness.) Therefore, be prepared to assert yourself in spite of whatever may be going on around you in the public venue:

...babies may be crying nearby,
...the barista may be barking out an order,
...groups of people could be loud and,
...there might be another interview going on at the table next to you

Overall, keep in mind that you want to give your interviewer a reason to be positive about you. Just as a director hopes that the next thespian to audition will be the perfect actor for the role, the interviewer is hoping that you will be a wonderful candidate – one he/she can envision on campus and one he can support in a write up.

Some simple tips:

- Smile - be upbeat
- Use examples to support answers
- Know specifically why you are a great fit for the school
- Engage the interviewer
- Listen to the interviewer
- Maintain eye contact with interviewer
- Have relevant questions for the interviewer
- Send him/her a thank-you note/email

Remember that the best interviews are conversations, not interrogations. It is not enough to simply answer the interviewer's questions with brief, terse responses. Show your interviewer that what he has to say is important – not just what you have to say is significant. Always keep your interviewer in your line of sight. Do not gaze off into the distance as you are thinking of an answer to a question. The interviewee should give the impression that he/she is enjoying the interview and the interviewer's company, even if it happens not to be true.

The Results

So, let's say you have succeeded. You have made a positive impression and the interviewer will write a stellar recommendation about your interaction that becomes part of your admissions file.

Your interviewer will be apprised of your admissions status -- your good or bad news -- acceptance, wait list, or denial. Our experience has shown that interviewers who support their candidates feel invested in the admissions status – they often feel their own nervousness about the results of their candidates' applications. Even though interviewers who have written supportive write-ups cannot always get their way, they feel elation along with you if your hard work in school and engaged conversation result in a letter of acceptance. So if you are fortunate enough to be accepted, let your interviewers know and let them celebrate with you.

CHAPTER 6

The Impressive You™ - Your Brand

❖ ❖ ❖

CHAPTER 6

The Impressive You™ - Your Brand

❖ ❖ ❖

Now that we have discussed the format and venue of the interview, let's get down to the meat and potatoes – the substance of what you hope to discuss in your one time meeting with a school of your choice. (Until you receive the letter of denial, every school to which you apply is a school of your choice.)

Remember, we have been trying to communicate that the interview offers you the one chance to convey that the college at issue is the perfect fit for you. The interviewee must arrive at the venue prepared to discuss his/her unique personal qualities. Those elements might include answers to the following personality inquiries:

- What do you feel strongly about?
- What are you most proud of?
- How have you made a difference?
- What is your key strength?
- What hardship have you endured and how have you recovered?
- What are your weaknesses?

These are **your** stories and enable the interviewer to get to know you. By highlighting these points during the conversation (no matter whether those direct questions are posed or not), you will be able to personalize and steer the interview. Your focused answers to these oft-repeated inquiries describe how your assets will contribute to the fabric of the school community.

Impressive You Exercise

Appendix 1 – The Impressive You – (all Appendices are located at the back of this book) is a useful tool which will help you – the candidate - prepare for an interview. This exercise will be helpful in crafting your Impressive You stories. Take 15 minutes to write down answers to the questions in *Appendix 1.* Gaining comfort and fluency with these responses will help strengthen the positive aspects of your conversation while minimizing any Achilles' heels you may have. Everyone has weaknesses and it is important to be able to acknowledge them to your interviewers. Your ability to show how you learned from hardships and how you have achieved your successes in spite of those setbacks reveals maturity and self-reflection.

Once you have learned the individual school's culture, you can explain how your personal attributes will contribute to that community and why you are a good fit for that institution. You do not **just** want to attend the school to take classes from its prestigious professors (many schools have them) or be in the country (most rural schools fit that bill) or walk in a big city…Everyone wants to do that.

What sets you apart from the next applicant? Why should the admissions committee accept you? Once you have identified your Impressive You points, you can field most of the interviewer's questions.

The Impressive You

Appendix 2 – The Impressive You Worksheet is one we use in working with clients to help further prioritize their talking points and create an Impressive You profile. You are welcome to try this exercise as well to name your talking points.

Develop **four key areas** which communicate your unique personal qualities. These are topics on which you want to focus during your interview. These are your key distinguishing talking points.

Now that you have identified what you will communicate to your interviewer, you are on your way to have an Impressive Interview. You know that whatever questions are posed, you will be sure to incorporate your unique personal qualities in the conversation.

Be Prepared with Questions of your Own

You must be prepared as well to ask the interviewer some questions about the university and how you will engage in its society if you are fortunate enough to be accepted. Do NOT ask your interviewer when she attended the school. (Bad…very bad.) Do ask the interviewer what her favorite aspect of the school is. That is a question that only she, as an alum or rep, can answer. It is not a question whose answer could be gleaned from the school's website, nor is it a sanctimonious fake salute to the school. It is part of the CONVERSATION. It shows your interest in the person with whom you are speaking and the school itself. It also, perhaps, provides you with possibilities you had not yet entertained as to how you could engage in the school if you are fortunate enough to be admitted.

Appendix 3 – Know Your Schools - insures that you are well equipped to ask intelligent questions. It covers the information you must know about the school to which you are applying. After completing *Appendix 3*, you can continue onto *Appendix 4 – Questions for your Interviewer.* The suggestions offered in *Appendix 4* are only recommendations. However, they give you an idea of how to frame school-specific questions rather than rely on unimpressive, generic talking points.

A successful interviewer we know (one who was accepted at schools and workplaces most of the time), once told me that the key to a good interview is to be sure that the interviewer leaves the meeting knowing something he did not know before you sat down together. That seems simple enough, but also makes a lot of sense.

Having learned from you, the interviewee, the interviewer will find the conversation unique and memorable. He can imagine your future interactions on campus. Remember – a college community is as much about what students learn from each other – beyond the classroom – as it is about the academic promise of an educational institution.

Assessment Grid

Before taking off to an interview, it is important to think about how the interviewer will evaluate you in comparison to other applicants. Our experience with admissions departments from years of writing up hundreds of applicants has revealed that assessments are usually based on four guiding points:

- Administration – the executive functioning of the candidate; how well the applicant coordinated the meeting time and if the student arrived at the correct venue and at the appropriate time;

- Appearance – self-explanatory; what efforts did the applicant put into presenting himself in neutral clothing – relaxed but not too relaxed
- Content – what the individual had to say;
- Communication – how well the applicant communicated his message; did he lose his train of thought? Ramble? Speak effectively?

By addressing these four areas, the interviewer is able to give an accurate summary of the applicant's potential. *Appendix 5 – Interviewer Evaluation Form* offers a more detailed examination of the evaluation process. Positive assessments of these four areas reveal maturity, forethought, and the type of high school senior who deserves a seat at a high level academic institution.

Share *Appendix 5* with your "practice" interviewer. That way you will offer the person a rubric by which to evaluate your interview and a tool which can be used to offer suggestions for improvement. In order to gauge your own performance, review *Appendix 6 – Mock Interview Self Assessment.* This will allow you to realize what you might be able to verbalize differently in the actual interview.

CHAPTER 7

The Interviewer's Helper - Paper-Perfect Profile™ Farewell to the Interviewer

❖ ❖ ❖

CHAPTER 7

The Interviewer's Helper - Paper-Perfect Profile™ Farewell to the Interviewer

❖ ❖ ❖

What is the Paper-Perfect Profile (PPP)?

You have completed your interview, discussed your Impressive You points, and are relieved that you have put the final punctuation point on your application. As you say good-bye and get the interviewer's contact information (so you can send a thank you note via email within a few hours,) you hand the interviewer your Paper-Perfect Profile. What is that?

The PPP is a one-page document that summarizes what you have discussed in your interview and makes the interviewer's life easy by supplying information for her write up. The PPP substantiates what you have discussed, reveals your potential, and expresses the reasons why the school of choice should select you for its freshman class. The summary is not simply a resume incorporating your academic achievements and scores. It focuses on the areas you outlined in the Impressive You - Your Brand Chapter. These are the topics you covered during your interview and serves as a helper or crib sheet, for the interviewers to refer to when they write an evaluation of you. You are trying to ensure that the information they communicate is accurate and a true reflection of you and your brand.

Many students hand a resume to the interviewer to supply him with data which may not have been discussed. However, the resume is an " easy" profile to hand off and usually has already been submitted as part of the written application. It includes information not pertinent to the interview and does not focus on what you want the interviewer to write about you – which may not be included in the written application! The PPP highlights your individuality, your goals, your experiences and what you bring to the table – to your college community and elements supporting your future success.

Appendix 7 – Paper Perfect Profile - offers a suggested outline for the PPP which will be helpful to you and your interviewer. Do not write a series of paragraphs. Try to keep the PPP specific, succinct, and a document you are proud to pass along.

CHAPTER 8

Champions' Circle - You Are Ready!

❖ ❖ ❖

CHAPTER 8

Champions' Circle - You Are Ready!

❖ ❖ ❖

Interview skills are tools that will be utilized during various chapters of your life. Although it is true that most young people have not had to prepare for an interview prior to the college application process, they must use this first opportunity to understand, digest and master the system by which to have an Impressive Interview. This book introduces students to the interview arena and offers strategies applicable to any application and interview process. As mentioned in Chapter 1, interview skills are life skills which must be called upon repeatedly for academic and career advancements.

It is always helpful to try to find a variety of questions that may be posed during interviews. Preparation is key. However, it is most important to know **what** you want to communicate during your one-on-one face time with a school representative. By engaging in the exercises for an Impressive You, you will define your potential to the prospective school, grantor, scholarship administrator and prospective boss. Once you have checked off the categories on *Appendix 8- Interview Checklist*, you should feel confident for your upcoming interview.

Don't take any chances with your interview. Practice and preparation are necessary. With too many applicants, colleges just need a reason to say "no." Don't let the interview write-up be that reason.

We leave you with representative, albeit fictitious, college interview write-ups. Some of the descriptions may seem harsh. However, that is the interviewer's job – alumni and staff alike. Interviewers are not asked to rubber stamp each candidate. They are asked to shed light on a candidate's viability at a particular school. After reading below, you will be able to decide for yourself which profile you hope will most closely parallel your own.

Interview Write-up:

Morgan was difficult to interview. Maybe she is just shy, but whatever the case, I had a hard time learning anything about what makes Morgan tick. Along with her ever-so-soft voice, Morgan did not seem to have much to say.

Morgan applied to Skylark because of the biology department. Morgan admitted that she had visited campus, but she did not speak of anything positive about her visit. She did tell me that she likes gymnastics and enjoys some of her volunteer work, but would not go into much more detail than that. So I still don't know why she likes the volunteer work or what she looks forward to when she wakes up in the morning. I could not discern any emotion or passion about anything in particular.

I got the feeling that Morgan was telling me what she thought I wanted to hear – about community service and sports. I am sure that whatever she told me is already revealed in her application and on her resume.

I asked Morgan if she had any questions for me. But the only thing she could come up with was a technical question about the biology department. I know some things about the bio department, but could not answer her state-of-the-art question.

I tried to stretch out the interview to a full 30 minutes. But that was a tall order and I had to let her go after 20 minutes, which is unusual for me.

I am sorry, but I cannot commend Morgan as I do not see what she will contribute to our campus or the student body.

Interview Write-up:

Brian is a nice young man. We actually had a decent conversation about his hobbies – sailing and online activities. He told me about the subjects he likes and disliked in school and his close relationship with his brother.

However, I do not endorse Brian as a candidate. Based on so many other students who I have interviewed over the years, he does not compare on many levels. He never mentioned any interest or participation in any community-oriented activities. I understand that he is close to his family, but I am hopeful that the students who are accepted to our campus have something to offer and will engage with fellow collegians.

Brian could not even articulate why he was applying to Skylark. He had solid thoughts, which he obviously shared, regarding some of the other schools he applied to. But he claimed that his interest in Skylark came from Naviance rather than personal investigation.

So, even though Brian seems nice, there are so few spots available at Skylark that I cannot see giving a seat up to Brian instead of to an applicant who shows real interest and passion in a field and our school.

Interview Write-up:

I liked Sam a lot and after the first 10 minutes of our meeting I thought I was going to love him. However, the conversation never made it to the love phase.

Sam is an extremely likable person – mature, well-spoken and articulate. He appeared to be totally sincere in his answers, rather than relating what he thought I wanted to hear which was refreshing.

Yet, given his maturity, I expected to hear all about his leadership and civic involvement, but that never materialized. Rather, he told me that he played on JV soccer and was part of a few clubs friends asked him to join. He mentioned that the group raised a ton of money for a charity. But when I asked how they went about doing so, he could only say that they had the usual bake sales and such. When we discussed what Sam liked to do to relax, he said video games – not very inspiring.

So, at the end of the day, I am torn about this candidate. I like him as a person and might be a well-liked addition to campus. However, it does not appear that he will bring any unique strength to the college community.

Interview Write-up:

Matthew was a pleasure to interview. It is no surprise that he admits that he works well under pressure.

He describes himself as honest and very loyal and does not change his perspective due to peer pressure. His teachers would say he is practical, knows what he needs to know and is organized. His friends call him determined, hardworking and they know that he puts school first. He is also a leader - organizing pick-up basketball and soccer games with his friends.

Ice Hockey is his sport and, having lived in Canada, he is a big hockey fan. He admires Joe Sakic, an Ice Hockey Hall of Famer known for his hard work and for being a play-maker. Matthew described how Sakic may not have had the talent of other players, but he was able to get the job done with set-up and that is what Matthew admires.

Matthew hopes to study bio-medical engineering along with a premed curriculum. His dream job is to become a doctor as he has always liked helping people. He enjoys learning – turning facts into something useful. Currently he tries to take information he learns in AP Bio and apply it to real life.

He is proud of his charity involvement in which his group is raising money to purchase clay pumps for South African communities. They purchased the initial pump, and are on their way to buying the second by raising $ by running a handball tournament and charging admission.

Matthew was great to talk to and he says that he is interested in the breadth of opportunities college will offer. We had a good dialogue about school and life in general. I truly enjoyed my time with him. He appears to be a pragmatic, well-organized student who will achieve his goals once they are set. I think that Matthew would make a vibrant addition to our school community and would bring with him the energy and enthusiasm that he conveyed to me in only a short time.

Interview Write-up:

Abigail seems like a fantastic candidate! Her maturity was evident from the moment I met her and she was articulate throughout the conversation. She had just come from rehearsal for her newest project as director of a play, and was exuberant about her involvement in the theatre. We discussed how she handles the stress of instructing other thespians and being on stage herself in front of an audience. She explained that the nerves of stage fright are more of a thrill and how lucky she feels she is to have the opportunity to perform in the first place.

Abigail has apparently done her research about our school and is excited to be considered for the program. She has investigated both the creative writing and acting programs and hopes to be able to join her interests in literature with bringing characters to life on stage. She hopes to be part of the community thespian troupes, some of which work on modifying behavior of young people in the school system. Abigail hopes to continue directing and act in productions on campus as well.

Abigail also seems to be engaged in learning for learning's sake. She was able to speak about complex connections between her literary studies and the stage. Her explanations were impressive and well communicated.

Our conversation flowed effortlessly and overall Abigail is a very personable woman who would transition easily to life at our university. I think Abigail would be able to make the best of her time at college and would be a fantastic addition to the class Of 20__!!!!

Practice, Practice, Practice

After reading this book, you are now aware that having an Impressive Interview requires preparation. The authors have provided you with knowledge to understand both the relevance of the interview in the College Admissions Process, and the steps that need to be taken in order to do your best when you interview. The insights and methodology outlined herein, are similar, albeit less personal, to what we cover when working with individual clients and workshop groups. *Appendix 8 – Interview Checklist* should be reviewed a number of weeks before your first scheduled interview. If you are touring colleges the summer before your senior year, and have arranged on campus interviews, be sure to review and complete the Interview Checklist. For alumni interviews, be prepared as soon as you have submitted your application as you will be contacted and must be ready to perform well as soon as the assigned alum makes contact. *Appendix 9 – Interview Day Checklist* should be reviewed the night before your scheduled interview. It can't hurt – can even be calming and helpful - to re-visit *Appendix 9* before each school's interview.

Your interviewers want to be positive about you. So help them be supportive in your application. Do your part to clearly communicate your story and strengths in a concise, genuine and authentic manner that resonate with your interviewer.

Now you can have that all important conversation, rather than an interrogation.

Good luck and happy interviewing!

APPENDICES

I-IX

APPENDIX I

The Impressive You™

Objective: To develop key points that describe the unique you!

The questions below help identify your personal qualities – "The Impressive You™." You should write about what you can most comfortably and clearly communicate. These topics represent who you are and what your value-add will be to the college community. Please answer the following questions in three sentences or less:

1. What is important to you?
2. What are you most proud of?
3. How did you make a difference?
4. What is your key strength?
5. Who do you admire and why?
6. Where do you see yourself in 5 years?
7. Why should a college accept you?
8. What will you give back to the college you attend?

APPENDIX II

The Impressive You™ Worksheet

Based on the answers completed in Appendix I, please develop four key points that communicate your unique personal qualities. These are areas that you are passionate about and in which you have excelled. They are your key distinguishing talking points:

1. Headline:
    b. Support

3. Headline:
    a. Support

3. Headline:
    a. Support

4. Headline:
    a. Support

APPENDIX III

Know Your Schools

1. Official college/university name and location -

2. School size, professor to student ratio and key majors -

3. Majors you are interested in and popular professors -

4. Housing and dining options -

5. What has been written in the news recently about the school?

6. Have any of your friends attended this university/college and what have they told you about it?

7. How does the college involve students in groups, extracurricular activities, or volunteer opportunities? Which of these areas appeal to you ?

8. What internship programs are offered?

9. Do they have a study abroad program - if yes, in which programs are you interested ?

10. Research the college's career guidance program –

11. In three sentences how would you describe the school ?

APPENDIX IV

Questions for Your Interviewer

Asking your interviewer questions underscores your interest in the school. This demonstrates that you have conducted research on the college and that you have been attentively listening throughout the interview. Develop 3 - 4 interview queries in advance and, as you are engaged in the conversation, you can add questions in response to what has been discussed if applicable.

Suggested question types:

- **Personal experience**

  - Do you have any advice for me as an incoming freshman?
  - What, if anything, would you have done differently during your time at _____?
  - What are your best memories from your time at ____ ?

- **Due Diligence**

  - Can a student only attend the abroad programs sponsored by ____ school or can one attend other opportunities?
  - I'm very interested in the internships. Do the alumni help with internship placements?

- **Response to what the interviewer has said**

    – Listen carefully to the interviewer and remember items discussed - for questions based on your conversation.

<u>Do Not Ask These Types of Questions:</u>

- Chances of gaining admission
- Details about academics
- Information contained on the website
- When did you graduate?

APPENDIX V

Interviewer Evaluation Form

Below please find areas often used to assess each applicant:

Administration:

- Was it easy to schedule the interview ?
- Did the applicant respond quickly to communication ?
- Did the interviewee arrive on time or early for the interview?

Appearance:

- Was student's appearance neutral ?
- Did it detract from the interview ?

Body Language:

- Did applicant display nervousness ?
- Did he look you in the eye ?
- Did she shake your hand ?
- Did he fidget ?
- Did he lean towards you to engage in the conversation ?

Communication:

- Could you hear the applicant ?
- Did she answer questions with a topic sentence and then support ?
- Did you feel that he was positive in his approach ?
- How would you describe the tone of the interview ?
- Did student display maturity ?

Content:

- Were the answers well thought out ?
- Did the candidate have knowledge of the school ?
- Did she appear prepared for the interview or did he wing it ?

Overall Rating:

- Was it an enjoyable interview ?
- Did you have a conversation or an interrogation ?
- Do you recommend this candidate for admission ?

APPENDIX VI

Mock Interview Self Assessment

Following your practice interview, please consider these questions and, based on your honest reaction to your dress rehearsal, modify your approach for the actual interviews.

How did I do on the interview?

What would I have liked to have answered differently?

What questions do I wish the interviewer had posed?

How do I hope to "do better" on in the actual interviews?

What were my strengths and weaknesses in the interview?

APPENDIX VII

Paper Perfect Profile™

Unlike a typical resume, often submitted with the written application, a PPP outlines areas on which you would like the interviewer to focus for his evaluation. The PPP summarizes "The Impressive You™" and suggests how you hope to be described to the Admissions Committee. It offers information beyond academic achievements and adds to what was included in your application - your goals, aspirations, personality, work ethic, etc. This can be your interviewer's cheat sheet for the interview write up.

- **Personal Statement**

- **Noteworthy Talents, Skills, and Interests**

- **Experiences and Community Service**

- **Athletics/Music/Unusual Course of Study/ etc.**

- **Academics and Honors**

APPENDIX VIII

Interview Checklist

- **Are interviews offered on campus or in your area?** Whatever the case, make sure you indicate that you want one to reveal that you are extremely interested in the school and willing to put in the time to have an interview.

- **If offered on campus, schedule your interview for the same day as your school visit (preferably after a tour and/or info-session).**

- **For alumni interviews,** which are typically conducted in local communities, your alumni interviewer will contact you to arrange a time and place.

- **Research the college.** Be prepared to answer detailed questions about the school and review any relevant news updates or blogs.

- **Create a list of 3 questions to ask your interviewer** – the answers to which you cannot find in school publications. This will impress the interviewer as you are asking for an opinion and input to your pertinent inquiries.

- **Review your Impressive You™ format.** These are the four key points you want to communicate during your interview, even if you adapt them to questions posed.

- **Develop your answers to potential key interview questions.** Review the sample questions contained in this book, and practice your answers to versions of these queries.

- **Conduct mock interviews with a friend or family member.** Review the interview tips and assessment grid outlined in this book.

- **Create your Paper Perfect Profile™ handout for your Interviewer.** The PPP will focus the interviewer's write up on your Impressive You Points.

- **Select an Impressive Interview outfit to wear.** Dress like you are going to visit an elderly relative. You do not want your outfit to be noticed. Business casual is always a positive.

APPENDIX IX

Interview Day Checklist

- **Double check the address for the meeting and your interviewer's name.** If you are meeting at Starbucks, or such, make sure you have the correct location–many chains have multiple locations in each town.

- **Arrive 10 minutes early.**
You never know how traffic will be and you do not want to be late.

- **Try to go to your interview alone.**
If your parents need to drive you to a local alumni interview, they should not appear at the venue. You must show that you are independent and can handle the interview on your own.

- **Dress "neutrally" so your appearance is not distracting to the interviewer.**
Do not chew gum or wear too much make-up. Have your outfit planned the day before so all you need to do is put it on!

- **Treat everyone you meet with respect.**
Leave a positive, upbeat impression with all of your contacts on or off campus.

- **Try not to let your "nerves" get the best of you; be yourself.** Because you have followed the advice and steps required to be prepared for your interview (as described in this book), you can relax and feel comfortable in the conversation. You should be calm because you know what you want to say and what you want to communicate about yourself. Try to enjoy the process……

- **Request your interviewer's contact information.** Ask for your interviewer's business card and make sure you follow-up with a thank you email and snail mail note.

About the Authors

❖ ❖ ❖

Peggy Nash Marx served as chairperson of a top New England college interview committee for many years. While working directly with admissions, she has managed the interview process for hundreds of diverse applicants. As a producer of corporate business meetings, Peggy has trained high-level executives on how to succeed in public speaking and interviews. Presently, Peggy owns two businesses – each of which helps individuals present themselves with confidence and pride. She is a magna cum laude graduate of Tufts University.

Kyrie O'Connor is a branding and marketing expert who has spent her career launching and building brands and businesses for Fortune 500 companies. She developed her flexible, entrepreneurial approach through classical marketing training at Kraft/General Foods, Cuisinart, Bally Shoes, BhS, Corning and London Fog. Along with CIC, Kyrie consults through her company, The Opportunity Team, and is a mentor/coach for the Yale Entrepreneurial Institute and the NYU Berkley Center for Entrepreneurship and Innovation. Kyrie has interviewed hundreds of students as chairperson of a top college interview committee. She graduated magna cum laude from Tufts and earned an MBA with honors from the Stern School at New York University.

Made in United States
Troutdale, OR
03/31/2024

18858720R00051